# STEAM IN SCOTLAND

## A PORTRAIT OF THE 1950s AND 1960s

First published in Great Britain in 2018 by
Pen & Sword Transport
An imprint of Pen & Sword Books Ltd
47 Church Street
Barnsley
South Yorkshire
S70 2AS

ISBN 9781526702173

Typeset by Aura Technology and Software Services, India
Printed and bound in India by Replika Press Pvt. Ltd.

Pen & Sword Books Ltd incorporates the imprints of Pen & Sword Archaeology, Atlas, Aviation, Battleground, Discovery, Family History, History, Maritime, Military, Naval, Politics, Railways, Select, Social History, Transport, True Crime, and Claymore Press, Frontline Books, Leo Cooper, Praetorian Press, Remember When, Seaforth Publishing and Wharncliffe.

For a complete list of Pen & Sword titles please contact
Pen & Sword Books Limited
47 Church Street, Barnsley, South Yorkshire, S70 2AS, England
E-mail: enquiries@pen-and-sword.co.uk
Website: www.pen-and-sword.co.uk

**Front cover:** See caption on page 44

**Title page:** A pair of immaculate CR 'Caley Bogie' 4-4-0s, Nos 54485 and 54486, stand at Forres on 21 May 1960 while working an Inverness to Perth train, after taking part in filming for the Railway Roundabout TV series. *(John McCann/Online Transport Archive)*

**Rear Cover (main picture):** LNER class D49 4-4-0 No. 62725 *Inverness-shire* climbs towards North Queensferry with an Edinburgh-bound local train on 4 August 1954. Built in 1928, this locomotive was in service for thirty years. *(Alan Sainty collection)*

**Rear cover upper right:** CR 4-2-2 No. 123 and GNSR 4-4-0 No. 49 *Gordon Highlander* prepare to leave Shotts, Lanarkshire, with a Scottish Industries Exhibition special from Princes Street station, Edinburgh, to Glasgow Central and Kelvin Hall. *(John McCann/Online Transport Archive)*

**Rear cover upper left:** See caption on page 161

# STEAM IN SCOTLAND

## A PORTRAIT OF THE 1950s AND 1960s

Kevin McCormack

PEN & SWORD
TRANSPORT

AN IMPRINT OF PEN & SWORD BOOKS LTD.
YORKSHIRE ~ PHILADELPHIA

GNSR class V (LNER class D40) 4-4-0 arrives at Craigellachie, Moray, on 2 April 1956 with a Speyside Line train from Boat of Garten. It will now proceed to the small engine shed and use the turntable. *(John McCann/Online Transport Archive)*

# Introduction

This colour photograph album covers steam in Scotland from the early 1950s to the end of Scottish steam in the mid-1960s and uses, to the best of my knowledge, images which have not previously appeared in print.

Although I am normally associated with railways around London, particularly the Western Region, since I spent most of the first twenty-five years of my life in Ealing, West London, I was actually born in Edinburgh and lived there in 1952/3 for that academic year. Our bungalow faced Kingsknowe station's level crossing, on the Carstairs-Princes Street line, and this was where my serious interest in trains started. To get to school, part of the journey involved taking local trains between Kingsknowe and Merchiston, usually hauled by a 2-6-4 tank. I was not aware of 'spotting books' with the numbers listed to underline so I made drawings and added the numbers of the locomotives I regularly saw, for example: 42204, 42269-73, 80026 and, on freight trains, 57559. I was very excited when I saw A1 Pacific No. 60152 *Holyrood* come through Kingsknowe (I have a blurred Box Brownie picture to prove it!) because this would normally be running on a line from Edinburgh Waverley.

After we returned to Ealing, I visited the Scottish capital most summers to stay with my maternal grandmother. This reinforced my liking for locomotives belonging to the Scottish Region of British Railway ('BR'), in particular the many pre-grouping classes which survived well into the 1960s and which did not normally stray south of the border. I was able to visit a large number of Scottish engine sheds (MPDs), usually with my mother in tow because she could talk her way round shed foremen, since I do not recall ever applying for a shed permit. With mother, we were never refused entry. In fact, on one occasion (at Thornton Junction shed) at the age of thirteen I was invited to drive a locomotive (Class J83 No. 68459) without even asking to go on the footplate. Sometimes we were provided with an escort and I remember that my mother was discomforted at Dawsholm (Glasgow) shed due to our escort taking a particular interest in her (to which I was completely oblivious as I was totally focussed on noting down engine numbers and taking photographs). She was therefore unhappy when I insisted on dragging her back the following year. However, I assured her that the chances of our meeting her unwelcome admirer again and he recognising her after a twelve month gap were minimal, but I was wrong. We were just walking along the road to the shed when we ran in to him, and he remembered her immediately, much to her annoyance!

Our annual visit inevitably meant a visit to my uncle's fiancée and sister which I always welcomed because they lived close to St Margaret's (Edinburgh) MPD which I would visit while they prepared afternoon tea. I can still vividly recall the excitement of 'copping' class K4 2-6-0 No. 61998 *Macleod of Macleod* in that 'smoky hole'. Sadly, visits during my 'train spotting' days coincided with the increasing proliferation of diesel multiple units (DMUs) replacing steam-hauled local services, many previously hauled in the Edinburgh area by pre-grouping 4-4-0s. Consequently, rows of these veterans could be seen stored at various sheds such as Bathgate, Polmont and Thornton Junction,

not forgetting the massive 'dump' of steam locomotives, both old and not so old, at Bo'ness. Many of Scotland's elderly machines carried strange names associated with novels written by Sir Walter Scott and I recall seeing such withdrawn hulks as *The Fiery Cross* at Thornton Junction, *The Lady of the Lake* at Haymarket and *Laird of Balmawhapple* at Bo'ness. Although this book concentrates on images of locomotives in service I have included a few views of named 4-4-0s in store because colour photographs of them are rare. Unfortunately, these do not include perhaps the three strangest named Scottish locomotives: *Jingling Geordie, Wandering Willie* and *Luckie Mucklebackit* !

Railway enthusiasts from across Britain flocked to Scotland during the final years of steam to enjoy two particular treats: seven years of main line operation by preserved steam locomotives in historic liveries (1958—1965) and four years of high-speed running (1962—1966) using otherwise redundant streamlined A4 pacifics. The latter's introduction on 3-hour expresses between Glasgow Buchanan Street and Aberdeen was a fitting swansong for an iconic locomotive class, although the honour of being Scotland's last steam withdrawals fell not to the

A4s or the many BR Standard classes built in the 1950s but to two class J36 0-6-0s dating from 1897 and 1900 respectively which remained in capital stock until June 1967.

BR's Scottish Region were much commended for their decision to restore to running order *Gordon Highlander, Glen Douglas,* the Jones Goods and the Caledonian Single, displaying the liveries of the pre-grouping Scottish railway companies they represent (the Great North of Scotland Railway (GNSR), the North British Railway (NBR), the Highland Railway (HR) and the Caledonian Railway (CR) respectively. The four locomotives were usually housed at Glasgow's Dawsholm shed (hence my visits there) between duties (normally enthusiast specials) and there was disappointment when these became static Glasgow museum exhibits. They were then joined by the only representative from the fifth major Scottish railway company, the Glasgow & South Western Railway (G&SWR), a 0-6-0 tank locomotive (No. 9) originally withdrawn in 1934 and acquired from the National Coal Board by BR for preservation in 1963. The Scottish Region is not however to be commended for its treatment of the HR 4-4-0 locomotive *Ben Alder* which was withdrawn in 1953 and stored for eventual preservation, latterly at Dawsholm, yet unexpectedly sold for scrapping in 1966.

A handful of other pre-grouping locomotives and a few post-grouping examples are also preserved, some of which are happily operational on heritage railways in Scotland. However, there are some notable omissions from the preserved ranks of Scottish classes which survived into the 1960s. For example, no 'Caley Bogie' 4-4-0s, several of which are depicted in this book, survive although a Belgian example derived from McIntosh's earlier Dunalastair II type is preserved in the 'Train World' museum at Schaerbeek in Brussels. The principal visual differences between this Belgian 18 class locomotive and a Dunalastair II are the full-width splashers and larger cab. This CR 4-4-0 'lookalike' was photographed by Bob Bridger at Leuven on 28 September 1980.

Let us now take a quick look at the development of railways in Scotland. Various amalgamations of small railway companies resulted in the creation of five main operators in the mid-nineteenth century, two of which were determined to be the first to provide a cross-border service into England. The Edinburgh-based NBR was formed in 1844 to provide a railway to the border at Berwick-upon-Tweed, which was achieved in 1846 when services from Edinburgh to Newcastle started in conjunction with the North Eastern Railway. However, the absence of bridges required passengers to 'de-train' in order to cross the River Tyne and River Tweed. On the other hand, the NBR's bitter rival, the CR, was able to provide a continuous train service between Carlisle and Glasgow in 1848 through co-operation with the London & North Western Railway, and also reached Edinburgh via Carstairs later in the same year. The NBR, determined to minimise any CR expansion to the west of its main line to Berwick, consequently set about building the 98-mile 'Waverley Route' from Edinburgh to Carlisle. The line reached Hawick by 1849 and Carlisle in 1862, the delay partly resulting from CR co-operation being required for entry into Carlisle itself. The opening of the Settle-Carlisle line by the Midland Railway gave a boost to the Waverley Route which also helped the G&SWR, formed in 1850 through a merger of the Glasgow, Dumfries and Carlisle Railway and the Glasgow, Paisley, Kilmarnock and Ayr Railway. The G&SWR, which had reached Gretna Junction in 1848, was then able to reach Carlisle via the CR two years later. So, by 1862, there were four Anglo-Scottish routes, two belonging to the NBR and one each to the CR and G&SWR.

Now for a few words about the remaining two big players, albeit the smallest two. These were the GNSR and HR which to some extent were also competitors. The GNSR was formed in 1845 with the aim of constructing a railway from Aberdeen to Inverness. The company went on to build several lines in north-east Scotland mainly in Aberdeenshire. The HR, formed by a merger in 1865, built its mainline from Perth starting westwards to reach the very top of the Country, avoiding Aberdeen (which was already reached by the CR from Perth taking an eastern course, as well as by the GNSR from the north and west).

It is also worth mentioning that at the railway grouping in 1923, the London, Midland & Scottish Railway (LMS) acquired the CR, G&SWR and HR while the NBR and GNSR became part of the London & North Eastern Railway (LNER).

The pictures in this album have been arranged on a roughly geographical basis starting on the eastern side of Scotland upwards from the English border, proceeding around the top of the Country and ending on the western side near the border. It is admittedly rather random but an index of locations has been provided at the end of the book which should help. I do not claim that the material presented is a comprehensive depiction of Scottish railways; my aim has been to concentrate on showing locomotives, preferably elderly ones, wherever they happen to be, since some are rarely seen in colour. Consequently, there are only a limited number of post-nationalization Standard classes depicted and not a diesel in sight! I have tried to concentrate on showing normal workings rather than railtours, but there are some of the latter, showing engines without headboards and with not too many people around. This is because railtours provided an opportunity to show all four Scottish preserved locomotives as well as some ordinary types normally seen in the 1960s in poor external condition but looking resplendent for enthusiast specials.

Most of the pictures used have been sourced from the Online Transport Archive, a charity set up to preserve photographs and moving images of transport. Other providers who have kindly allowed me use of their photographic material are Jim Oatway and Bruce Jenkins. Alan Sainty has kindly given me access to his collection and I have Bob Bridger to thank for the use of Charles Firminger's pictures. There are even some of my colour slides included but most of my Scottish pictures taken from 1958 are monochrome because of the poor weather that seemed to plague my visits to Scotland in August/early September, although, judging by the sunny photographs in this book, others had better luck.

I hope readers will enjoy this nostalgic glimpse of the Scottish railway scene in the 1950s and early-mid 1960s before the closure of so many lines as the 'Beeching Axe' was wielded and remaining services were dieselised.

*Kevin R. McCormack*
*Ashtead, Surrey,*
*December 2016*

**Above and right:** A short branch just under 2 miles long ran from Beattock to the spa town of Moffat. Opened in 1883 and subsequently acquired by the CR, the line was closed to passengers on 6 December 1954 and to freight on 6 April 1964. In this undated view at Moffat taken before 29 December 1962, which was when CR 0-4-4 tank No. 55234 was withdrawn, the locomotive is seen attached to a mineral wagon at the goods shed before assembling a freight train and preparing to leave from the station platform. The awning has clearly seen better days! *(RWA Jones/Online Transport Archive - both)*

Moving across from the CR to the NBR, this next view is taken at Eyemouth in East Lothian, the terminus of a 3-mile branch from Burnmouth on what is now the East Coast Main Line (ECML) north of Berwick. The branch was constructed as a light railway and opened in 1891, with the NBR initially taking a lease before purchasing the line. Closure came on 5 February 1962 and this scene shows LNER J39 0-6-0 No. 64917 hauling the final freight train out of Eyemouth and running alongside the Eye Water on 3 February 1962. *(Charles Firminger)*

Turning now to the NBR's Waverley Route from Carlisle to Edinburgh which was built to serve cloth manufacturing towns such as Hawick, its closure was highly controversial. This caused implementation to be delayed and enabled several farewell enthusiast specials to be operated over the line. One such special ran on 18 April 1965 hauled by Gresley A4 pacific No. 60031 *Golden Plover* which is seen here at Galashiels. This is now the penultimate station on the new Borders Railway, opened on 6 September 2015, which currently terminates at Tweedbank and may eventually reach Hawick and even Carlisle once more. *(Charles Firminger)*

This is Carstairs, a former CR station on the present West Coast Main Line (WCML) where this picture was taken on 21 July 1961. The subject is the doyen of the LMS Coronation class pacifics, No. 46220 *Coronation*. In the year of its construction this locomotive set a steam record of 114mph on 29 June 1937 but the record was quickly broken by Gresley's A4 pacific *Mallard* in the following year when 126mph was reached. *Coronation* was one of several members of the class which were initially streamlined to enable the LMS to compete with the LNER A4s on Anglo-Scottish expresses. This particular locomotive exchanged identity with No. 6229 *Duchess of Hamilton* in 1939 for the latter to make an American tour as *Coronation,* before reverting to its original number and name when No. 6229, masquerading as No. 6220, returned. *(Jim Oatway)*

Carstairs is also a junction with a former CR line to Edinburgh on which I used to live when aged 5-6 years. My parents and I, plus dog, would frequently walk up Kingsknowe Road South across the Lanark Road and down to the site of Hailes Platform on the Balerno Loop which left the Edinburgh-Carstairs line at Slateford and rejoined it at Ravelrig. We would then walk along the line and through the tunnel to Colinton station where this picture of a railtour headed by standard class 3 2-6-0 No. 78046 was taken on 19 April 1965. On the left are the derelict remains of a 12-ton CR carriage built at St Rollox in 1890. The Balerno Loop was built to serve the various mills on the adjacent Water of Leith and opened in 1874. It was closed to passengers on 30 October 1943 and to freight on 4 December 1967. *(Charles Firminger)*

The MPD which served what the locals called the 'Caley' station at Edinburgh (officially Princes Street station) was Dalry Road, much the smallest of Edinburgh's three principal engine sheds. Taking on coal on 18 July 1958 is a resplendent visiting Stanier Jubilee 4-6-0, No. 45624 *St. Helena* from Crewe North shed. Built in 1934, this engine was withdrawn in November 1963. Four members of the class of 191 locomotives have been preserved, but not the nominal pioneer, LMS No. 5552 *Silver Jubilee,* named to commemorate HM King George V's twenty-five years on the throne in 1935. In any case this was not the genuine doyen of the class. The name was bestowed upon No. 5642, a newer locomotive, which was duly renumbered 5552! *(Ian Dunnet/Online Transport Archive)*

We are still at the former CR Dalry Road shed, this time on 17 July 1958, and find a locomotive that seems to have lost its way because it is a former NBR class K locomotive allocated to St Margarets (Edinburgh). The Glens became LNER class D34 and this is No. 62471 *Glen Falloch* which was built in 1913 and withdrawn in July 1960. Dalry Road MPD closed on 3 October 1965 and was quickly demolished. It was a cramped depot and had lacked a turntable since 1934. Locomotives either visited a nearby triangle for turning purposes or used the turntable at Princes Street station, just over a mile away to the east. *(Ian Dunnet/Online Transport Archive)*

Replacing earlier structures, Princes Street station was completed in 1893 and the Caledonian Hotel above opened ten years later. By the 1960s, the station was considered redundant and surviving services were transferred to the former NBR Waverley station. Closure occurred on 6 September 1965 and this picture was taken a few months earlier, on 20 April 1965. It depicts the 10.10am train to Birmingham hauled by Standard Britannia class pacific No. 70002 *Geoffrey Chaucer* from Carlisle (Kingmoor) shed, piloted by LMS Fairburn 2-6-4 tank No. 42058 allocated to Carstairs. *(Charles Firminger)*

A resplendent St Margarets-based J37 0-6-0, No. 64608, hauls empty stock from Craigentinny sidings bound for Edinburgh Waverley on 2 July 1960. Craigentinny depot, near Portobello, was set up by the NBR in 1914 for servicing and cleaning carriages, a role it continues to perform today. Some five weeks after this picture was taken, No. 64608 was noted at Carlisle hauling a stopping train to Hawick, demonstrating that these powerful locomotives could be found working passenger services. This engine enjoyed a long working life, entering service in 1919 and being withdrawn at Dundee Tay Bridge MPD in August 1966. *(Ian Dunnet/Online Transport Archive)*

Gresley A4 pacific No. 60023 *Golden Eagle,* allocated to Gateshead MPD, passes Craigentinny carriage sidings on its way from Newcastle to Waverley station on 2 July 1958. This locomotive was the fifth member of the class of thirty-five to be built and the first not to include the word 'silver' in its name. Entering service in October 1936, No. 60023 was withdrawn in October 1964. *(Ian Dunnet/Online Transport Archive)*

At first glance this enormous station could be mistaken for Perth but it is in fact Leith Central, terminus of a 1.25-mile branch from Edinburgh Waverley which opened in 1903 and closed on 7 April 1952. The fact that the now demolished station still existed when this photograph of preserved D40 No. 49 was taken on 19 April 1965 was due to its use as a DMU depot from 1952 to 1972. The NBR deliberately built this 'folly' to demonstrate its superiority over the CR which also had a circuitous branch from Princes Street station to North Leith and was threatening to build a more direct line tunneling under Edinburgh to reach Leith. *(Charles Firminger)*

At the open roundhouse (once covered) on the north side of St Margarets MPD on 22 May 1958 the driver of NBR class F/LNER J88 No. 68320 of 1904 vintage struggles to turn his locomotive. Looking on are NBR class G/LNER Y9 0-6-0 saddletank No. 68102 and LMS Fowler 0-6-0 tank No. 47162. One Y9, No. 68095, which was a St Margarets engine, has been saved and is on display at the Scottish Railway Preservation Society (SRPS) museum on the heritage Bo'Ness & Kinneil Railway. St Margarets closed on 1 May 1967. *(Ian Dunnet/Online Transport Archive)*

With the ECML in the foreground, NBR class J/LNER D30 4-4-0 No. 62421 *Laird O'Monkbarns* simmers on the south side of St Margarets MPD on 1 March 1959. There were forty-three NBR J class locomotives (D29s and D30s) which, with their 6ft 6in driving wheels and large tenders, were designed as express engines capable, for example, of travelling non-stop between Edinburgh and Carlisle. No. 62421, seen here with a snowplough attached, was built in 1914 and, along with No. 62426 *Cuddie Headrigg,* was the last to remain in service, being withdrawn in June 1960. The class was given names taken from Sir Walter Scott's novels and were nicknamed 'Scotts'. *(Ian Dunnet/Online Transport Archive)*

Approaching Edinburgh Waverley station from the east on 3 July 1958, class V3 2-6-2 tank No. 67617 hauls a Gresley parcels van past the surviving southernmost walls of Calton Jail, opened in 1817 and largely demolished in 1930. Allocated to St Margarets, No. 67617 started life as a Gresley V1 in 1931 and was rebuilt with higher boiler pressure in 1957 to become a V3. Eighty-two V1s were built, of which seventy-one became V3s and with the final batch being built as V3s, the combined class totalled ninety-two engines. Designed for heavy suburban passenger work, these locomotives were displaced by diesel multiple units (DMUs) from 1960 and none survives. *(Ian Dunnet/Online Transport Archive)*

Here is another view of the eastern end of Waverley station, this time with a southbound ECML train departing. The date is 16 August 1954 and the locomotive is Gresley A3 pacific No. 60089 *Felstead* from Haymarket (Edinburgh) MPD. This engine was built in 1928 and named after the Epsom Derby winning racehorse of that year. There were seventy-eight members of the A3 class, excluding the first one which was later rebuilt to become the first A1. No. 60089 was withdrawn in October 1963 but a single example has been preserved which needs no introduction: 60103 *Flying Scotsman*. *(Alan Sainty collection)*

There was a tradition at some major railway stations in Great Britain to have resplendent station pilots specifically allocated to that particular duty and Edinburgh Waverley was one such example. Here, on 14 June 1958, we see Holmes NBR class D/LNER J83 0-6-0 tank No. 68481 from Haymarket MPD waiting at the western end of Waverley station close to the Waverley Bridge, with Edinburgh Corporation sightseeing coaches standing above. No. 68481 was the last member of a class of forty of this type and was built by Sharp Stewart in 1901. It was withdrawn on 12 February 1962 but diesels had already been allocated to Waverley station pilot duties from March 1959. *(Ian Dunnet/Online Transport Archive)*

A smart looking Thompson B1 4-6-0, No. 61330, accelerates out of the Mound tunnel on its departure from Waverley with a local train on 26 September 1956. The grubby light engine on the left is Peppercorn A2 pacific No. 60529 *Pearl Diver* which, like the B1, dates from 1948. This locomotive was named after the 1947 Derby winner which was the first French-trained horse to win this race for thirty-three years. The Mound is an artificial hill connecting the Old Town with the New Town following the filling in of the Nor Loch which enabled Princes Street Gardens to be formed. *(Ian Dunnet/Online Transport Archive)*

Two westbound departures from Waverley on 16 August 1954 race each other towards the tunnel under Lothian Road and Princes Street station that emerges at Haymarket. Princes Street itself can be seen on the left beyond West Princes Street Gardens and in the distance on the right are the spire of the Scott Monument and the clocktower of the North British Hotel (now called the Balmoral). The local train on the left is headed by class D34 4-4-0 No. 62475 *Glen Beasdale* while another local passes the foot of Edinburgh Castle rock with a powerful class V3 2-6-2 tank, No. 67672, in charge. *(Alan Sainty collection)*

Compared with St Margarets, Haymarket MPD tended to house more glamorous locomotives, eg streamlined A4 pacifics, but, as evidenced in the next sequence of pictures, more prosaic types could also be found there. A locomotive type less commonly seen in Scotland was the Gresley GNR class H4/LNER K3 2-6-0. One hundred and ninety-three of these express goods engines, notorious for rough riding, were built between 1920 and 1937. This example, No. 61854, seen on 4 July 1959, has probably brought a freight up the ECML as its home shed is Tweedmouth, Berwick, just south of the Border. No. 61854 was built in 1925 and withdrawn in December 1962. *(Ian Dunnet/Online Transport Archive)*

The first member of the D34 'Glen' class, No. 62467 *Glenfinnan,* simmers at Haymarket MPD on 30 June 1958. Thornton Junction, its home shed, appears to be keeping this veteran passenger locomotive, dating from 1913, in presentable condition and it lasted another two years before being withdrawn. *(Ian Dunnet/Online Transport Archive)*

The first of the six-strong K4 class, No. 61993 *Loch Long*, entered service in 1937 and is depicted here at Haymarket on 4 July 1959. The locomotive was withdrawn in December 1962 but I nearly caused its demise in 1960! In the Introduction I briefly mention being invited to drive class J83 No. 68459 at Thornton Junction shed. The crew asked me to stop the locomotive outside the shed doors for them to put it inside. Then I was to halt the engine by using the steam brake. I turned the handle furiously at the appointed time but we still banged into the locomotive behind. This happened to be *Loch Long* on blocks under repair with some driving wheels removed. Only quick thinking by the crew in grabbing the handbrake prevented disaster! *(Ian Dunnet/Online Transport Archive)*

Still at Haymarket on 4 July 1959 we now see a Gresley D49 4-4-0, No. 62709 *Berwickshire*. This class of seventy-six locomotives, built between 1927 and 1935, was designed for light express duties and the engines were named either after shire counties or fox hunts. At one time there were three variants with different types of valve gear. This example was an unaltered D49/1 type, as is the preserved example, No. 62712 *Morayshire*. This is currently on the Bo'ness & Kinneil Railway and probably owes its survival to the fact that it became a stationary boiler for a short time at Slateford Laundry following its withdrawal. The D49s were the first LNER-designed passenger class. *(Ian Dunnet/Online Transport Archive)*

Here is a view of Peppercorn class A1 pacific No. 60152 *Holyrood* photographed on 26 June 1958. Following on from the Thompson prototype (No. 60113 *Great Northern*) which was a 1945 rebuild of the first Gresley pacific dating from 1922 forty-nine Peppercorn A1s were constructed in 1948–9 (Nos. 60114–60162) and, since none was preserved, a further A1 (No. 60163 *Tornado*) has been built which was completed in 2008. Only five A1s entered service in Scotland (all delivered to Haymarket) including 60152, which did not receive its name until 1951. The locomotive was withdrawn in June 1965. *(Ian Dunnet/Online Transport Archive)*

**Above:** We leave Haymarket MPD with a view of long-term resident D11 4-4-0 No. 62690 *The Lady of the Lake* on 15 March 1959. Although seemingly out of use, the locomotive was not officially withdrawn until July 1961. Standing behind is ex-CR 0-4-4 tank No. 55165 which spent some seven weeks allocated to Haymarket before returning to Dalry Road. *(Ian Dunnet/Online Transport Archive).* **Right upper and lower:** Entering West Lothian, we see two D30 Scott class 4-4-0s in store at Bathgate on 12 April 1959, both withdrawn at Hawick in December 1958. They are No. 62432 *Quentin Durward* and No. 62422 *Caleb Balderstone*. The NBR class Js comprised two types, non-superheated and superheated, with the latter sometimes known as 'Superheated Scotts'. However, the LNER put them into two separate classes, D29 and D30, although the last two D29s were actually superheated and became prototypes for the D30 class. *(Paul de Beer/Online Transport Archive- both)*

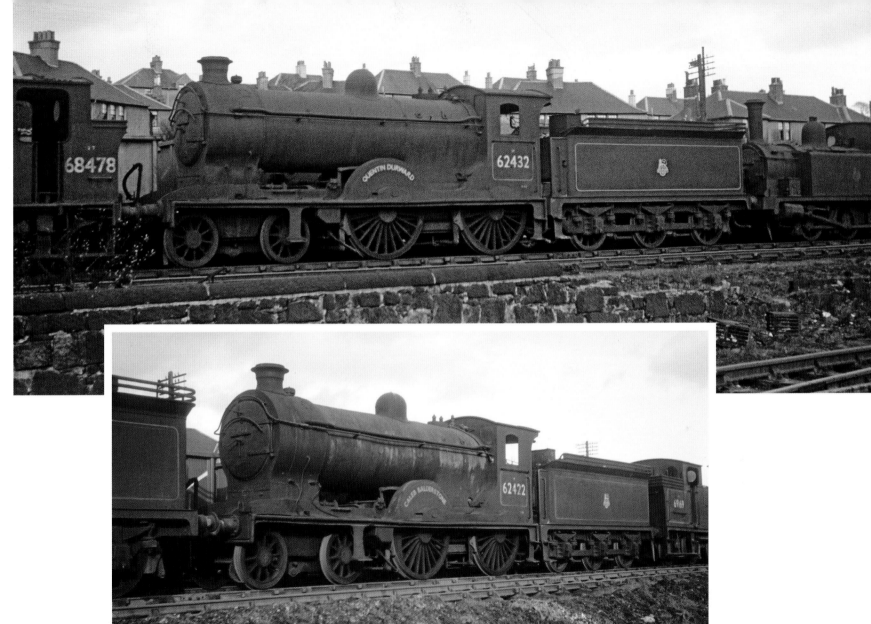

Here is another Scott class 4-4-0 cast out from Hawick and dumped at Bathgate while a scrap merchant was found. Seen on 12 April 1959, this Reid NBR class J/LNER D30, No. 62428 *The Talisman,* was built in 1914 and withdrawn in December 1958. There seems to have been some confusion over the correct name to apply to the engine because in the periods from December 1931 to February 1938 and May 1940 to March 1947 the definite article was missing and it ran as *Talisman. (Paul de Beer/Online Transport Archive)*

In the mid-1960s Bathgate MPD became a magnet for enthusiasts because it still used a small fleet of Victorian tender engines (J36s) to service the nearby collieries. When I visited the shed in early September 1965 to see the J36s (arriving on my Honda 50 motorcycle, having driven up from West London on A roads as it was banned from motorways because it was 49cc!) there was not a J36 in sight and I feared the worst. However, the kindly shed staff told me that the three active ones were all at work and gave me the exact locations (sadly now forgotten!) and here is one that I followed out of a colliery, No. 65297 dating from 1897. *(Author)*

The other J36s that I pursued on my motorbike were Nos 65267, pictured in another colliery, and 65282. The latter was photographed bringing a loaded coal train past Lower Bathgate signal box before continuing to Bathgate Upper (see page 38). *(Author - both)*

No. 65297 has now returned to shed and is having its fire dropped while sister engine No. 65267, built in 1892 and withdrawn in November 1966 after achieving nearly seventy-five years of service, is being coaled up from the timber coaling stage ready for the following day's duty. Bathgate MPD was closed to steam on 31 December 1966 by which time the three aforementioned J36s had been withdrawn although this still left one at Thornton Junction and another at Dunfermline, making these Victorian relics Scotland's last steam locomotives to be withdrawn. *(Author)*

**Opposite top:** Class J36 No. 65282 (built 1896) pauses at the former Bathgate Upper station with a loaded coal train. This station closed in January 1956 but still looks tidy almost ten years later. **Opposite lower:** When the three working J36s returned to base, one (No. 65282) had been put into the shed before the other two (Nos 65267 and 65297), thereby denying me a photograph of all three together. Expressing my disappointment the obliging engine crew pulled it out so that I could take this shot! **Above:** Polmont shed on 20 July 1961 is host to class J37 No. 64537 and a J38 in steam, plus three withdrawn locomotives: J72 No. 69014, J35 No. 64532 and J83 No. 68448, all former St Margarets residents destined for the Bo'ness dump. *(Author - 2; Jim Oatway)*

Being prepared for work on 20 July 1961 at Grangemouth MPD is Holmes NBR class C/LNER J36 0-6-0 No. 65306, dating from 1899. The class, which totalled 168 machines, was built between 1888 and 1900. Withdrawals took place, excepting an earlier accident victim, over a prolonged period: from 1931 to 1967! All were rebuilt between 1913 and 1923 with side-window cabs and slightly larger boilers, with twenty-five being called up by the Government for service in France during the First World War. These received names associated with the War on their return, one such example being *Maude,* No. 65243, which has been preserved by the SRPS. *(Jim Oatway)*

The ECML crosses the Firth of Forth using the magnificent Forth Bridge (opened in 1890 and viewed here from the ferry). Immediately beyond is North Queensferry where, on 19 April 1957, St Margarets-based Gresley class V2 2-6-2 No. 60894 is pictured steaming through on a freight.

*(John McCann/Online Transport Archive - both)*

Fife, like West Lothian on the south side of the Firth of Forth, was a major coal mining area and this view **(above)** on 19 April 1957 depicts Dunfermline-based N15 0-6-2 tank No. 69135 hauling a loaded coal train near North Queensferry. **Right:** Gresley 'A3' Pacific No. 60099 *Call Boy* powers up the steep incline between Inverkeithing and North Queensferry on its way to the Forth Bridge and Edinburgh on 4 August 1954. This Haymarket-based locomotive was built in 1930 and named after the racehorse which won the 1927 Derby. The photograph, and the following three, together with the front cover, were all taken on the same day depicting trains heading to Edinburgh. Seen on either side of the tracks, they are all exiting the same rock formation which is adjacent to the southbound carriageway of the A90 where an entry slip road from Hope Street is located. *(John McCann/Online Transport Archive; Alan Sainty collection)*

**Above:** This Reid D30 Scott class 4-4-0 is No. 62431 *Kenilworth* from Thornton Junction MPD dating from 1914 and withdrawn in 1958.
**Right:** Here we see Thompson A2/3 Pacific No. 60519 *Honeyway* which was based at Haymarket from new in February 1947 until October 1961. The A2 class consisted of several variants, many of which were allocated to Scottish depots because, in order to be more economical, they needed to be given heavy duties and, with stiff gradients, the Edinburgh-Dundee-Aberdeen route was found to be ideal for them.
*(Alan Sainty collection - both)*

Now for a very different type of Scottish 4-4-0, an English design produced by Robinson for the Great Central Railway (GCR). These LNER class D11 engines were called 'Improved Directors' (compared with the previous D10 class) and about the only feature they had in common with NBR 4-4-0s was being named after literary characters created by Sir Walter Scott. Following the grouping of the NBR into the LNER in 1923, a plea was made to Gresley for some new express passenger locomotives for ex-NBR services so, for expediency, twenty-four 'Scottish Directors' were built in 1924. These were based on the GCR design, but had lower cab roofs and boiler mountings to suit the NBR gauge. This example, No. 62675 *Colonel Gardiner,* lasted until 1959. *(Alan Sainty collection)*

After the Forth Bridge, North Queensferry and the brief rock formation the ECML enters another tunnel before reaching Inverkeithing station where this picture was taken. The date for this and the following six pictures is early September 1965. The train is a southbound empty stock working hauled by St Margarets-based Gresley 2-6-2 No. 60955. Designed for express freight services but, as a scaled down version of an A3 pacific, equally suited to express passenger services 184 of these powerful, fast locomotives were built between 1936 and 1944. Eight were named, including the prototype, *Green Arrow,* which is the only preserved example. *(Author)*

Inverkeithing was where the line to Perth separated from the ECML to Dundee and Aberdeen. It also had a goods yard to the north of the station. Shunting in the yard on the date of my visit was Dunfermline's much loved J36, No. 65288, a product of 1897 which remained in stock for seventy years, not being withdrawn until June 1967. The yard was busy during my brief time there, with four freight trains leaving, two hauled by J37 0-6-0s (see page 50), one behind a B1 4-6-0 and another behind a WD (see opposite). *(Author)*

Scotland had War Department (WD) 2-10-0s as well as the normal 2-8-0s but this is one of the latter, photographed only because it was unusually presentable. Seen alongside Inverkeithing goods yard and about to head a freight southwards, No. 90534 was built by Vulcan Foundry of Newton–le-Willows, Lancs in 1943. Nine hundred and thirty-five of these machines were built, of which 932 were sent abroad for use in the Second World War. When this ended all but 184 returned to these shores and 733 were acquired either by the LNER or subsequently by BR. One has been preserved, having been repatriated from Sweden, and is on the Keighley & Worth Valley Railway. *(Author)*

**Above:** LNER class J37 0-6-0 No. 64571 pulls out of Inverkeithing yard with a freight, leaving class member No. 64623 to follow on later, both engines being allocated to Dunfermline. One hundred and four of these ex-NBR locomotives were built between 1914 and 1921 for heavy freight work and were a superheated version of the older J35 class. They were powerful and very successful, but they were also heavy, thereby lacking the versatility of the lighter J36s which, despite their venerable age, were more suitable for use on tracks such as those of the National Coal Board. **Right:** No. 64623 has now returned to Dunfermline MPD after completion of its working day. *(Author - both)*

**Upper:** Brighton-built Standard class 4 2-6-4 tank No. 80060 arrives at Larbert, near Falkirk, with a local train from Stirling possibly heading for Glasgow on 20 July 1960. *(Ian Dunnet/Online Transport Archive)*
**Lower:** J36 No. 65288 is getting ready for bed at Dunfermline MPD. *(Author)*

We are now turning further inland and taking the former NBR route from Inverkeithing to Perth, stopping off at Stirling. After many pages of NBR locomotives, it is time to see some more from the CR although both companies served Stirling, albeit from different directions. This is a CR Pickersgill 72 class locomotive, No. 54501, built by the North British Locomotive Company of Glasgow in 1922. The engine looks dead, yet smoke seems to be rising from its chimney. While this could be an optical illusion caused by an unseen locomotive behind No. 54501 being in steam, the picture was taken on 20 July 1961 and the engine was not withdrawn until December 1961. *(Jim Oatway)*

Returning to the NBR for a picture taken on 11 April 1959, this is D30 (Scott) class 4-4-0 No. 62436 *Lord Glenvarloch,* a resident of Dunfermline shed, which, judging by its headlamp code, has probably brought a local train from there to Stirling. No. 62436 was built in 1915 and was one of the last of the class to remain in service, being withdrawn two months after this photograph was taken. *(Paul de Beer/Online Transport Archive)*

The station pilot at Stirling on 19 July 1958 was locally-based CR Standard Passenger class 0-4-4 tank No. 55222, designed by McIntosh and built in 1914. There were seventy-eight locomotives of this type and one has been preserved (No. 55189) by the SRPS and is kept on the Bo'Ness & Kinneil Railway. No. 55222 was withdrawn in September 1961. *(Ian Dunnet/Online Transport Archive)*

Undoubtedly one of the most successful British locomotive designs was the Stanier Black Five. No fewer than 842 of these mixed traffic engines were constructed between 1934 and 1951 and eighteen have been preserved. No. 45158 *Glasgow Yeomanry* was one of only five named (the name of one allegedly only lasted from 1942-1944), the names being those of Scottish Regiments. No. 45158 was built in 1935 and was shedded at Balornock (better known as St Rollox, Glasgow) when this picture was taken on 16 April 1959. *(Paul de Beer/Online Transport Archive)*

This is what NBR class K/LNER class D34 Glen 4-4-0s should look like! Formerly BR No. 62469 *Glen Douglas,* this locomotive was restored to its pre-grouping state in 1959, receiving its former NBR identity (No. 256) and bronze green livery. The locomotive then took part in the programme of special trains operating from 5–19 September 1959 in connection with the Scottish Industries Exhibition at Kelvin Hall, Glasgow. For these duties it was joined by the other three restored Scottish engines plus No. 3440 *City of Truro* from BR Western Region. No. 256 was then used to haul other specials such as this one on 13 April 1963 when it was photographed at Rumbling Bridge on the Alloa-Kinross (Devon Valley) line which closed to passengers on 15 June 1964. *(Charles Firminger)*

The same railtour depicted on the previous page has now proceeded to Auchtermuchty in Fife where this overhead view of the cab of No. 256 *Glen Douglas* was taken. This Reid 4-4-0 was built by the NBR at their Cowlairs Works located at Springburn, Glasgow, in 1913 and last worked from Keith depot prior to being selected for preservation. Auchtermuchty was on the Fife and Kinross Railway which ran between Kinross and Ladybank. The line closed to passengers on 5 June 1950 but remained open to freight until 5 October 1964. *(Charles Firminger)*

We now move across to the East coast and visit Kirkcaldy, so-called linoleum capital of the world (until linoleum was superseded by floor tiles and fitted carpets). The picture dates from around August 1966 and depicts a northbound train heading for Perth or Dundee which has just pulled out of the station and is passing Kirkcaldy NBR signal cabin with its forty-four-lever mechanical frame. In the background, in Station Road, is the Caledonia Works of Barry, Ostler & Shepherd, linoleum manufacturers, which closed about 1964. The train is hauled by Gresley A4 Pacific No. 60034 *Lord Faringdon,* the last of this famous locomotive class to be built. It was withdrawn on 24 August 1966, very shortly after this picture was taken. *(Author's collection)*

**Left upper:** Clearly it is hard work turning a class B1 4-6-0 by hand unaided on Thornton Junction's turntable. The date is 19 July 1961 and the engine is Vulcan Foundry-built No. 61178 from Haymarket MPD. **Left lower:** In the previous year, I saw class D34 4-4-0 No. 62484 *Glen Lyon* at Thornton Junction before it saw further service at Hawick. Here is a close-up of one of its splashers showing its name and builder's plate. Although the locomotive started life with the NBR in 1919, the LNER has replaced the builder's plate with one carrying its own company name which was normal practice. **Above:** This general view of Dundee (Tay Bridge) MPD also dates from 19 July 1961. The locomotive nearest the camera is A2 Pacific No. 60527 *Sun Chariot*. *(Jim Oatway - all)*

These are two pictures taken on 20 May 1961 at Dundee (Tay Bridge) MPD, which closed to steam on 1 May 1967. **Above:** Seen previously on page 41, Gresley V2 2-6-2 No. 60894 spent its entire working life from 1940 to 1962 based in Edinburgh, fluctuating between St Margarets and Haymarket. **Right:** Gresley class J38 0-6-0 No. 65931 stands over the ash pit next to the coaling tower. This Thornton Junction locomotive belonged to a class of thirty-five powerful freight engines which were all based in Scotland. They were the last LNER class to remain intact, being withdrawn from December 1962 to April 1967, and BR's last Gresley locomotives to operate. *(Charles Firminger - both)*

The date is still 20 May 1961, as it is for the next four pictures, and what a fine day that turned out to be, weatherwise and for Caley Bogie lovers! Pickersgill CR class 72 4-4-0 No. 54500 looks beautiful as it stands at Dundee West station at the head of an enthusiasts special watched by some admiring local schoolboys. The station was the CR's Gothic-style terminus of the former Dundee and Perth Railway which was closed on 3 May 1965 to make way for a bypass, although the line itself is still open. Luggage trolleys such as the two in the foreground made convenient seats for trainspotters! *(Charles Firminger)*

Now for another Caley Bogie, No. 54486, seen previously on page 1. This is a particularly interesting picture because it depicts a boy in mid-air and another in the cab! The location is Kirkbuddo, Angus, an intermediate station on the CR's Dundee and Forfar Direct Line. Passing through some sparsely populated areas, the route was not well patronised and passenger services ceased on 10 January 1955. Freight services were withdrawn from the upper (Forfar) end of the line on 8 December 1958 and the remainder of the line closed on 9 October 1967. *(Charles Firminger)*

**Above:** Forfar station closed to passengers on 4 September 1967 and the last train to run was a farewell special on 5 June 1982. There is now no trace of the station. In happier times, Caley Bogie No. 54465 prepares to leave Forfar with an enthusiasts' special on 22 April 1962.
**Right:** Looking somewhat less resplendent than on page 64 after the accumulation of two months of grime, No. 54500 simmers outside Forfar MPD on 19 July 1961. The station has vanished but remarkably the engine shed lives on today in commercial use. *(Charles Firminger; Jim Oatway)*

This is Leyhill, Angus, with the same railtour seen on page 66 hauled by Caley Bogie No. 54465 standing at the northern platform. The southern platform is visible in the foreground on the left. The platforms were staggered, being located on either side of the level crossing. Leyhill was situated on the former Arbroath and Forfar Railway which was later taken over by the CR. Passenger services were withdrawn on 5 December 1955 and freight on 25 January 1965. *(Charles Firminger)*

Viewed from the signal box, LMS Ivatt class 2 2-6-0 No 46463 piloting No 46464 prepare to haul a railtour at Elliot Junction. The station was on the Dundee and Arbroath Joint Line which is currently the main line from Dundee to Aberdeen but there is now no trace of the station which closed on 4 September 1967. The Dundee and Arbroath Railway was absorbed by the CR but in a rare example of inter-company co-operation the CR gave the NBR joint ownership of the line to its terminus at Arbroath and then running rights over the CR beyond there to enable the NBR to reach Aberdeen following the latter's building of the Tay Bridge in 1878. Elliot Junction was where a branch to Carmyllie, closed to passengers in 1929 and to goods traffic in 1965, diverged from the mainline. *(Charles Firminger)*

Moving further up the east coast we reach Aberdeen station, known up to 1952 as Aberdeen Joint station, reflecting the fact that it replaced the previous Aberdeen Railway/CR Guild Street station and the Great North of Scotland (GNSR) Waterloo station. **Above:** This view depicts Gresley class V2 2-6-0 No. 60851 and Standard class 4 2-6-4 tank No. 80020. **Right:** D34 class 4-4-0 No. 62479 *Glen Sheil* undertakes station pilot duties on 5 April 1958. This 1917-built locomotive was withdrawn in May 1961. *(Alan Sainty collection; Paul de Beer/Online Transport Archive)*

Standing outside Aberdeen station on 31 July 1955 is the only Gresley A3 pacific to be fitted with A2-type smoke deflectors, No. 60097 *Humorist*, which it received in 1947. This locomotive was the first of its class to be fitted with a Kylchap blastpipe and double chimney but problems with drifting smoke obscuring the driver's view led to various smoke-lifting experiments being carried out on this engine. *(John McCann/Online Transport Archive)*

Also on 31 July 1955, station pilot duties at Aberdeen were in the hands of Reid class N15 0-6-2 tank No. 69128. There were ninety-nine of these locomotives, classified by the NBR as class A and by the LNER as classes N14 and N15. No. 69128 was based at Aberdeen (Ferryhill) MPD at the time of this picture being taken. Built in 1910 the locomotive gave fifty-two years service. Note the shunter's step beneath the cab and bunker and the handrail above. *(John McCann/Online Transport Archive)*

This is a picture taken on 30 September 1960 which should interest the Bon Accord Locomotive Society. This organisation has not preserved the A1 pacific No. 60154 *Bon Accord* (if they had there would have been no need to have built *Tornado* !). Instead, the Society has preserved this little 0-4-0 saddletank named *Bon Accord*. Built by Andrew Barclay & Sons in 1897(Barclay Works No. 807), this engine belonged to Aberdeen Gas Works and hauled coal wagons from Aberdeen docks to the gas works in Cotton Street until its replacement by a diesel in 1968. *Bon Accord* had its wheels and motion covered because some street running was required. It is currently based at the Royal Deeside Railway, see next caption. *(John McCann/Online Transport Archive)*

Gresley K2 2-6-0 No. 61779 storms out of Aberdeen on 19 April 1954 with the 8.11am train to Ballater. The Deeside Railway, the Deeside Extension Railway and the Aboyne & Braemar Railway all built sections of the Ballater branch between 1853 and 1866 and these companies were absorbed by the GNSR in 1875/6. This scenic 12.5-mile line was often used by royalty and visiting heads of state on their journey to and from Balmoral, but, as a victim of the Beeching Axe, was closed to passengers on 28 February 1966 and dismantled. The heritage Royal Deeside Railway operates a 1-mile section from Milton of Crathes and is working on an extension to Banchory. *(John McCann/Online Transport Archive)*

Aberdeen had two MPDs, the CR one at Ferryhill which closed to steam on 31 March 1967 and this one, Kittybrewster, which belonged to the GNSR. In the foreground is NBR class D34 4-4-0 No. 62480 *Glen Fruin,* a longtime resident of Kittybrewster, and standing behind is a an Atlantic tank. The type of mechanical coaling plant seen in the background was rarely found in Scottish MPDs, although Haymarket had a similar structure. Kittybrewster shed closed to steam on 12 June 1961 and the site has been cleared. *(Alan Sainty collection)*

It is hoped that readers like D40 4-4-0s because most members of the class that survived into the 1950s will appear in several of the pages which follow! We start with three views of No. 62279 *Glen Grant* on 7 November 1953 at Peterhead 'shed' (an apt description – MPD does not seem appropriate!). No. 62279, the penultimate member of the class of twenty-one which was numbered 62260–62280, entered service in 1920 and was withdrawn in May 1955. *(John McCann/Online Transport Archive)*

**Above:** No 62279 *Glen Grant* on the Peterhead turntable and **Right**: having its ash emptied. Peterhead was the eastern coastal terminus of a branch from Maud Junction, where the GNSR line from Aberdeen continued to Fraserburgh on the north coast. The Peterhead branch closed to passengers on 3 May 1965, the introduction of diesel multiple units (DMUs) having failed to save either of the lines to Peterhead or Fraserburgh. Freight services to Peterhead ceased in 1970. The locomotive could have been named after a well-known distillery which was founded in Speyside by the Grant brothers in 1840 but there is an actual Glen Grant although this has been described as more of a ravine than a gentle valley. *(John McCann/Online Transport Archive - both)*

The Beeching Axe decimated Scottish branches and one such victim was the former GNSR Tillynaught-Banff line in Aberdeenshire which was closed to passengers on 6 July 1964 and to freight on 6 May 1968. **Left upper:** BR class 2 2-6-0 No. 78045 arrives at Tillynaught with the 9.50am from Banff on 29 December 1962, clearly a freezing day, and returns, **left lower**, with the 11.20am from Banff, where it is seen, with a mixed train, leaving Ordens Halt. **Above:** Sister engine, No. 78054, stands in Banff station which, until 1928, was named Banff Harbour.

*(Charles Firminger - two; Alan Sainty collection)*

Moving slightly south westwards we come to Keith Junction, now just known simply as Keith, which is on the Aberdeen-Inverness mainline. Originally, this is where the GNSR from Aberdeen met the HR from Inverness. There was also a GNSR branch to Dufftown and Craigellachie. A heritage operation, the Keith & Dufftown Railway, operates a DMU service between Dufftown and Keith Town, with ambitions to extend to Keith (Junction). This shot taken on 28 May 1955 features class D40 No. 62265 (former GNSR class V) at Keith Junction. This was one of the earlier Pickersgill non-superheated engines, none of which received names. Built in 1909, it lasted until January 1957. *(John McCann/Online Transport Archive)*

Class D40 No. 62273 *George Davidson* pulls out of Keith shed on 9 November 1953. This was the first of Heywood's eight superheated GNSR class F machines, all of which carried names, and was built in 1921 and withdrawn on 31 January 1955. George Davidson was the third and final General Manager of the GNSR and was appointed to the newly formed LNER at the Grouping but died in harness in 1928 at the relatively early age of fifty-seven. *(John McCann/Online Transport Archive)*

Like D40 No. 62265 on page 82, No. 62268 was another of the Pickersgill non-superheated engines (former GNSR class V), none of which bore names. Built in 1910 and withdrawn in July 1956, this view depicts the engine outside Keith shed on 1 August 1955. William Pickersgill's railway career started with the Great Eastern Railway and he was appointed locomotive superintendent of the GNSR in 1894. He moved from there to the CR in 1914. *(John McCann/Online Transport Archive)*

The last shot at Keith shed was another taken on 9 November 1953 when No. 62273 *George Davidson* (see page 83) was raising steam alongside Gresley class K2 2-6-0 No. 61779. Belonging originally to Great Northern Railway class H3, this locomotive was built just one month after No. 62273 and was one of a class of sixty-five K2s built between 1914 and 1921 (excluding some rebuilt K1s which were added to the class). All the original K2s were initially allocated to English sheds but over the years thirty were transferred to Scotland of which thirteen were named after Lochs. No. 61779 was un-named and withdrawn in May 1960. To protect against inclement weather, all the Scottish K2s received side-window cabs.
*(John McCann/Online Transport Archive)*

We leave Keith with a view of class D40 No. 62269 shunting in the yard there on 9 November 1953. This locomotive, another of the Pickersgill non-superheated type, was withdrawn in September 1955. Eighteen of the twenty-one D40s survived to become BR locomotives in 1948, with twelve being withdrawn from Keith and the remaining six from Kittybrewster. *(John McCann/Online Transport Archive)*

Travelling westwards from Keith Junction on the surviving mainline from Aberdeen to Inverness, we come to Elgin. There were originally two stations here, the HR's Elgin West (now plain Elgin) and the GNSR's Elgin East. This closed on 6 May 1968 following the closure of the Lossiemouth branch to passengers in 1964 and the Moray Coast Line and Craigellachie branch in 1968, these routes succumbing to the Beeching Axe. On 9 November 1953, class D40 4-4-0 No. 62267 was found on a freight leaving Elgin yard. Built in 1909, the locomotive was withdrawn in August 1956. *(John McCann/Online Transport Archive)*

Here is the famous D40, No. 62277 *Gordon Highlander,* seen at Elgin on 10 November 1953. Built by the North British Locomotive Company in 1920, this locomotive was the last of the class to remain in service, being withdrawn on 23 June 1958. It was then sent to the former GNSR Works at Inverurie for overhaul (where ten D40s were built, but not 62277) and re-entered service as GNSR No. 49 for use on specials, its inaugural trip being on 13 June 1959. It was withdrawn in June 1966 and transferred to the Museum of Transport in Glasgow. In this view, the tender is devoid of any ownership markings and has a sheet at the rear of the cab to keep out the cold on the hilly routes on which it was used. *(John McCann/Online Transport Archive)*

This is a view of the former GNSR shed at Elgin (East) on 30 July 1955 which was built in 1902. It is not to be confused with the former Morayshire Railway's nearby shed which is now a Grade B listed building constructed in 1863 and later taken over by the GNSR. In this view, class D40 No. 62264 is about to enter the shed which is now home to bin-lorries and other vehicles belonging to Moray Council. Dating from 1900, the locomotive was withdrawn in March 1957. *(John McCann/Online Transport Archive)*

**Above:** We leave Elgin with a view of the preserved HR 'Jones Goods' 4-6-0 No. 103 built in 1894. **Right:** No. 103 was kept busy in late August 1965 for the HR Centenary, running several trips with the restored CR coaches (no HR ones were available). The CR coaches, seen at Tomatin, between Aviemore and Inverness, and now on the Bo'ness and Kinneil Railway, are Brake Corridor Composite coach No. 464 built in 1923 and Third Class Corridor Compartment coach No. 1375 from 1921. The guard is wearing replica HR uniform. *(Harry Luff/Online Transport Archive - all)*

**Left:** Craigellachie was on the slightly circuitous GNSR line from Elgin to Keith and was the junction for the Strathspey line to Boat of Garten and Aviemore. In this view, Standard class 4 2-6-0 No. 76107 has brought a train in from Elgin while GNSR No. 49 *Gordon Highlander* waits in the Strathspey platform. **Above:** Also arriving from Elgin is CR class 113 4-4-0 No. 54472, complete with snowplough attached, on 30 March 1959. This locomotive was built in 1916 and was a slightly smaller version of the CR class 72 Caley Bogies seen earlier in this book. *(Alan Sainty collection; John McCann/Online Transport Archive - two)*

**Left upper:** No. 62277 *Gordon Highlander* stands at Craigellachie with a Boat of Garten train on 24 July 1957 with Geordie Scott, the train guard, the fireman (unknown) and driver Jimmy McPherson. **Left lower:** On the same day, the photographer, John McCann, stands on the footplate of *Gordon Highlander,* in between Jimmy McPherson and the fireman. **Above:** Class D40 No. 62271 has arrived at Craigellachie from Boat of Garten on 28 May 1955. *(John McCann/Online Transport Archive - all)*

GREAT NORTH OF SCOTLAND RAILWAY.

**NOTICE** AS TO **TRESPASS.**

PURSUANT TO THE GREAT NORTH OF SCOTLAND RAILWAY ORDER 1909.

*The Great North of Scotland Railway Company hereby give notice to all persons not to trespass upon any of the lines of Railway belonging or leased to or worked by the Company. And notice is hereby further given that any person who shall trespass upon any of such lines of Railway shall on conviction be liable to a PENALTY not exceeding FORTY SHILLINGS.*

ABERDEEN.
1ST October 1909.

T.S. Mackintosh,
Secretary.

**Left:** After arriving at Craigellachie, No. 62271 visits the engine shed to use the turntable before returning to the station to haul the next train to Boat of Garten. The trespass notice at Craigellachie was photographed some three years later, on 7 April 1958, thirty-five years after the GNSR ceased to exist. **Above:** Having been turned, No. 62271 is ready to leave with the 2.55pm train to Boat of Garten on 28 May 1955.

*(John McCann/Online Transport Archive -all)*

There were nine intermediate stations on the Speyside line and this is Blacksboat, the fourth one from Craigellachie. Opened by the GNSR in 1863 and closed when passenger services were withdrawn on 18 October 1965 (the introduction of diesel rail buses in the 1960s failed to save the line), the building is now a two-bedroom detached house, advertised for sale in 2015 at offers over £195,000. The Speyside Way walk now occupies the trackbed. However, this is how the station looked on 2 April 1956 when No. 62271 steamed in on its way to Boat of Garten.

*(John McCann/Online Transport Archive)*

The next stop after Blacksboat was Ballindalloch where No. 62271 is seen on 28 May 1955, working the 2.55pm from Craigellachie.
The locomotive, which was withdrawn in December 1956, was built at the GNSR Works at Inverurie in 1914. The Works closed in 1970 but its name lives on in football circles. In the same year that the Works opened (in 1902), the Inverurie Loco Works Football Club was formed and is still very active today. *(John McCann/Online Transport Archive)*

**Above:** Having emerged from a hard winter on the Speyside Line and still with snowplough attached, D40 No. 62265 hauls a freight near Ballindalloch in April 1954. **Right:** Grantown-on-Spey used to have two stations with the same name and both closed to passengers on the same day, 18 October 1965. This is the Speyside Line one, the penultimate station before Boat of Garten. On 20 May 1960, preserved D40 No. 49 (62277) *Gordon Highlander* returned to its old haunts in connection with a *Railway Roundabout* TV filming of the line. *(John McCann/Online Transport Archive - both)*

No. 62271, in rather worse external condition than previously seen, waits at Boat of Garten on 1 August 1955 (it looked much better in the following year!). The heritage Strathspey Railway has preserved this station which is roughly half way between the line's current starting point at Aviemore and its temporary northern terminus at Broomhill. The Strathspey Railway is not operating over the GNSR Speyside line but over the HR line from Boat of Garten to Forres which was closed to passengers simultaneously with the Speyside line. The heritage railway is working its way northwards from Broomhill to Grantown-on-Spey (not the one on the Speyside line). *(John McCann/Online Transport Archive)*

The D40 4-4-0s were the GNSR's principal express passenger locomotives but as loadings increased the LNER decided that larger engines were necessary for this work. Consequently, the Company drafted in twenty-five Great Eastern Railway (GER) Holden B12 4-6-0s (GER class S69) to take over and the D40s were relegated to secondary duties. The Scottish contingent was withdrawn between 1946 and 1954, replaced by B1s, and No. 61502, seen here bringing a freight into Boat of Garten goods yard on 10 November 1953, was one of the last two, succumbing in April 1954. Class member No. 61572, the sole British inside-cylindered 4-6-0 to be preserved, lives on the North Norfolk Railway. *(John McCann/ Online Transport Archive)*

Evening sunshine on 10 November 1953 illuminates both the wonderful scenery and the locomotives which are standing outside Boat of Garten shed. No. 61502 has deposited its freight wagons and a D40, No. 62274 *Benachie* is also in view. Ironically, the D40s just outlived their replacements, the B12s, with 1921-built *Benachie* lasting until September 1955. Bennachie (spelt 'nn') is a range of hills in Aberdeenshire.

*(John McCann/Online Transport Archive)*

This Caley Bogie, No. 54466, pictured at Aviemore on 31 March 1956, belongs to the sixteen-strong CR Pickersgill 113 class, a slightly older (built 1916) and, in terms of cylinder size, marginally smaller version of the later CR 72 class seen elsewhere in this book. Aviemore was the junction on the HR where the line to Inverness via Carr Bridge diverged from the route to Forres via Dava and the GNSR Speyside line. The footplate crew on No. 54466 are taking no chances with the weather as they hide behind a large tarpaulin. *(John McCann/Online Transport Archive)*

**Above:** The ubiquitous D40 No. 62271 stands on Aviemore's turntable on 31 March 1956. The shed closed in 1965 when passenger services on the Forres route were withdrawn and has since been taken over by the heritage Strathspey Railway which uses it as its workshop and maintenance facility. The turntable featured in this picture was scrapped and has since been replaced by the one from Kyle of Lochalsh.

**Right**: Against the backdrop of the Cairngorms, a train headed by two Stanier 'Black Five' 4-6-0s prepares to leave Aviemore on 22 April 1957. The station is still open, being situated on the Perth-Inverness mainline and since 1998 the Strathspey Railway has been able to use Platform 3 for its services to Boat of Garten and Broomhill. *(John McCann/Online Transport Archive - both)*

Broomhill is mentioned on page 106 as being the current terminus of the Strathspey Railway. As the first station north of Boat of Garten on the line to Forres, this is how it looked on 21 April 1957. Following closure of the route on 18 October 1965, the buildings seen here were demolished but the Strathspey Railway have constructed replica buildings on the surviving platform, complete with a replacement two-armed signal, opening it on 31 May 2002. The purpose of the lower quadrant signal shown here was for passengers to activate it to request the train to stop.

*(John McCann/Online Transport Archive)*

Two 'Black Fives' haul an express up Dava Summit (1,052ft), roughly half way between Boat of Garten and Forres, on 21 September 1957. The first vehicle is an ex-HR Travelling Post Office, one of three built in 1916 (see inset picture of an example, No. M30322, photographed on 6 April 1958). The 36-mile line between Aviemore and Forres was particularly demanding, not just as a result of the gradients, but also because of the propensity for extreme weather. On 9 February 1963 a passenger train on Dava Moor hauled by two diesel locomotives became buried in frozen snow drifts thirty-foot deep which had to be removed using dynamite. It was three weeks before services resumed.

*(John McCann/Online Transport Archive - both)*

Britain's first 4-6-0 locomotive, HR 'Jones Goods' No. 103, stands at Forres with the two preserved CR carriages. Designed by David Jones (the HR's Locomotive Superintendent) and built by Sharp Stewart, No. 103 was the first of a class of fifteen such locomotives which were the most powerful main line engines in the country at that time. No. 103 was withdrawn in 1934 for preservation and re-entered service in 1958, operating until 1966. In this view it was running a series of shuttles between Inverness and Forres in late August/early September 1965 in connection with the HR Centenary. *(Harry Luff/Online Transport Archive)*

Caley Bogies Nos 54485 (at front) and 54486 set off from Forres for Perth on 21 May 1960 in connection with a filming for the *Railway Roundabout* TV programme (see also page 1). Forres station is no longer a junction following the closure of the southbound Dava route to Boat of Garten and Aviemore but remains in use for trains running east to west between Aberdeen and Inverness via Keith and Elgin.

*(John McCann/Online Transport Archive)*

After using the turntable in front of the shed roads HR No. 103 steams through the triumphal arch at Inverness MPD on 21 April 1962. The arch disguised a water tank, part of which is visible on the left. The shed was a semi-roundhouse, initially with twenty-one roads and extended on both sides to create thirty-one roads around 1875 to cope with the HR's increased locomotive requirements as the Company expanded its operations. It is possible that the arch was intended to be the entrance into a complete roundhouse, but roughly two-thirds of the circle was the extent of building and the arch stood on its own. The shed closed on 30 June 1962 and the site was cleared in the following year. *(Charles Firminger)*

Inverness was the headquarters of the HR and the station was originally opened in 1855 as the western terminus of the Inverness and Nairn Railway. This company was taken over by the Inverness and Aberdeen Joint Railway (IAJR) in 1858 following the extension of the route beyond Nairn. In 1865, the IAJR amalgamated with the Inverness and Perth Junction Railway, giving birth to the HR. By 1959, diesels were beginning to replace steam in the Highlands and CR McIntosh Standard Passenger Tank No. 55226 dating from 1914, seen here at Inverness on 15 April 1959, would shortly be transferred to Perth from where it was withdrawn in September 1961. *(Paul de Beer/Online Transport Archive)*

A stranger comes to the north of Scotland in the form of a Western Region 0-6-0 pannier tank, seen here preparing to leave The Mound with a mixed train to Dornoch. In the 1950s the Dornoch branch had been operated by two HR 0-4-4 tanks but these expired in 1957 and 1958 and the most suitable replacements were deemed to be two comparatively new (1951-built) lightweight pannier tanks. These were No. 1646 which arrived in February 1957 and No. 1649 (the example seen here) which crossed the border in July 1958. The branch closed on 13 June 1960 along with The Mound station, the main purpose of which had been to act as the junction for the Dornoch branch, and the locomotives were withdrawn two years later. *(Harry Luff/Online transport Archive)*

No. 1649 takes water at The Mound. The 7-mile long Dornoch branch was largely funded by the Duke of Sutherland. Although worked by the HR it was independent, being owned by the Dornoch Light Railway Company until its absorption into the LMS at the Grouping in 1923. The fact that the line was built as a light railway meant that only locomotives with a light axle loading could be used, but they had to be powerful enough to haul mixed trains. For the opening ceremony in 1902 the Duke of Sutherland's 1895-built personal locomotive *Dunrobin* was used. This engine, which the Duke was able to operate on the national rail network until nationalisation in 1948, was purchased by Beamish Museum in 2012 and is currently in the process of being returned to steam. *(Harry Luff/Online Transport Archive)*

There was a small engine shed at Dornoch used for overnight stabling but the main depot where the Dornoch locomotives were kept and serviced was at Helmsdale, The shed was situated alongside the station but this picture of Pickersgill Caley Bogie No. 54495 shows the locomotive against the backdrop of the goods shed. The 14.5-mile line from Dunrobin to Helmsdale was built by the third Duke of Sutherland and opened in 1870. Some eights months later the HR took over the running of the line following that Company's completion of the railway south of Dunrobin (now called Dunrobin Castle). North of Helmsdale the line continues to Georgemas Junction where it diverges for Thurso and Wick. *(Harry Luff/Online Transport Archive)*

An example of what is generally regarded as Stanier's least successful standard locomotive design stands at Georgemas Junction alongside a row of cattle wagons on 22 September 1959. Allocated to Wick, No. 40150 belonged to a class of 139 3P 2-6-2 tanks and was built in 1937. The last survivors were withdrawn in December 1962, including this engine. The tracks entering from the left carried trains from the south, eg Inverness, and the locomotive is standing on the line to Thurso which curves away northwards in the background. Trains from the south destined for Thurso therefore had to reverse whereas those bound for Wick continued eastwards through the station. *(Ian Dunnet/Online Transport Archive)*

A route which has been reprieved at least twice from closure and is hopefully now safe is the ex-HR line from Dingwall to Kyle of Lochalsh. With most trains running from Kyle to Inverness, these take passengers on a wonderful scenic ride across Scotland from the west to the east coast, an 80-mile journey taking approximately two hours, forty minutes. Kyle station is situated on the banks of Loch Alsh and consists of an island platform carrying the main station building (still in use), with sidings on both sides. This photograph taken in May 1957 shows CR 0-4-4 tank No. 55216 built in 1912 attached to a van at the end of platform 2 facing towards Inverness. *(Jim Oatway)*

This view at Fort William shed in July 1959 shows one of the two Beaver-tailed Observation cars used on the West Highland line being turned prior to being attached by a J36 0-6-0 to the end of a Mallaig-bound train. The two cars were built in 1937 for the launch of the LNER Coronation streamlined express train (coinciding with the Coronation of King George VI) which ran between Kings Cross and Edinburgh until its permanent withdrawal at the start of the Second World War. In 1956, the vehicles (E1719E and E1729E) were transferred to Scotland and were rebuilt in 1958 with a more angular rear window to improve visibility. They remained in service on the West Highland route until 1968 and both are now in the hands of the heritage Great Central Railway. *(Bruce Jenkins)*

On 26 September 1960 the photographer travelled on the magnificent West Highland line (Mallaig Extension) from Fort William to the fishing town of Mallaig. **Left:** The heavy passenger train, which includes freight vans, heads westwards after Glenfinnan station hauled by Peppercorn K1 2-6-0 No. 62012 piloting a Standard class 4 2-6-0. **Above:** Against the backdrop of the Moidart Mountains, the mixed train arrives at Arisaig, the penultimate station before Mallaig. This ex-NBR route is arguably the most scenic in Great Britain and, in addition to the normal diesel services, tourist steam train services have operated during summer months since 1984, a demanding assignment for the locomotives as they handle the steep gradients and tight curves on the line. *(John McCann/Online Transport Archive - both)*

Moving further southwards down the west coast of Scotland we come to Oban, reached from a junction at Connel Ferry which was also the start of a much longer branch to Ballachulish. The former CR route to Oban, which started life as the Callander and Oban Railway, is still open west of Crianlarich (but closed eastwards to Callander). However, Oban engine shed closed on 12 March 1962, coinciding with the withdrawal of services on the Ballachulish branch. This view of Pickersgill 3P 0-6-0 No. 57667 at the shed, belonging to CR class 300 which comprised forty-three engines built 1918–20, was taken in May 1957. *(Jim Oatway)*

Also photographed in May 1957 was 0-4-4 tank No. 55263 at Ballachulish, ready to depart for Connel Ferry. The main purpose of building the branch was to transport slate from the local quarry, visible behind the station building (the latter now in use as a medical centre). In the distance, the top of the Pap of Glencoe mountain can be seen. The full name of the station was Ballachulish (Glencoe) for Kinlochleven and the line closed on 28 March 1966. The locomotive was built by Nasmyth Wilson in 1925, one of ten ordered by the LMS developed from the earlier McIntosh CR 439 class. *(Jim Oatway)*

Moving inland along the Callander and Oban line on the now closed section east of Crianlarich (Lower), Killin Junction is reached. This was the point where the delightful 4-mile branch to Killin and Loch Tay joined the main line which Killin folk originally believed would serve their village but, when proved wrong, decided to build their own branch. Although operated by the CR on a revenue-sharing basis, the independent Killin Railway Company passed direct to the LMS at the Grouping. Against the backdrop of the Grampian Mountains, with Ben Lawers prominent, McIntosh CR No. 55204, dating from 1910, prepares to climb the 1 in 50 gradient from Killin to Killin Junction on 23 May 1961.

*(John McCann/Online Transport Archive)*

In this view the Killin branch train is in the hands of CR Standard Goods 0-6-0 No. 57276, a veteran 'Jumbo' built in 1885 and withdrawn in November 1959. Passenger services to the original terminus at Loch Tay were withdrawn on 9 September 1939 when the boat services to Kenmore ceased although the extension remained open because the engine shed, together with coal and water facilities, was located there. The remainder of the line closed completely after 27 September 1965 which was a few weeks earlier than the planned closure date of 5 November, owing to a landslip at Glen Ogle on the Callander line. This route had been due to close concurrently with the Killin branch and was consequently also closed prematurely. *(Harry Luff/Online Transport Archive)*

Callander station is a hive of activity in this view dating from 23 May 1961 featuring two Stanier Black Five 4-6-0s hauling a train towards Stirling, the leading locomotive being No. 44881. Whereas the line north of Callander closed prematurely due to the aforementioned rock fall at Glen Ogle, Callander station itself succumbed on the scheduled closure date of 5 November 1965. The station site was quickly cleared and is now a car park but the iron bridge seen here which is carrying the Ancaster Road remains in use. *(John McCann/Online Transport Archive)*

Whereas some passenger tank engines in the late 1950s/early 1960s, such as the ex-CR 439 class 0-4-4 locomotives, could still be found looking smart, this was not normally the case with goods engines. An exception, however, was Perth's station pilot, McIntosh CR class 782 No. 56347, which belonged to a class of 138 3F shunting engines built between 1898 and 1913 (this one dates from 1912). Photographed on 23 April 1962, only three months before its withdrawal, No. 56347 has just taken over an enthusiasts special at Strathord, on the former CR route from Perth to Forfar, in order to travel over the 3-mile light railway to Bankfoot which closed to passengers in April 1931. The line remained open to freight until 1964. *(Charles Firminger)*

The next station north of Strathord was Stanley Junction where the HR line to Inverness diverged from the CR line to Forfar. One of the intermediate stations north of Stanley Junction was Ballinluig, itself a junction for the 8.5-mile Aberfeldy branch. This branch closed completely on 3 May 1965, as did Ballinluig on the mainline. **Above:** Pickersgill CR class 431 No. 55239 built in 1922, one of four such engines designed for banking, stands at Ballinluig in June 1961. **Right:** McIntosh CR class 439 0-4-4 tank No. 55217 runs round its train in June 1961 at Aberfeldy in preparation for the return journey to Ballinluig while considerable activity takes place on the platform. *(Alan Clayton/Online Transport Archive - both)*

Here is another picture at the HR Aberfeldy terminus, with CR 0-4-4 tank No. 55218, dating from 1913, having just arrived from Ballinluig. The station signal box and small engine shed can be seen in the background. A large car park now stands on the site of the station and the buildings at the two intermediate stations, Grandtully and Balnaguard Halt, have also been removed. Like so many closed Scottish branch lines, the Aberfeldy line offered a scenic journey as part of the route ran alongside the River Tay but so-called economies arising from the replacement of steam by diesel power failed to save the line from the Beeching Axe. *(Harry Luff/Online Transport Archive)*

Moving south to Perth, No. 62671 *Bailie MacWheeble* is destined for oblivion, having been officially withdrawn some six weeks before this picture was taken on 19 July 1961, although, judging by its rusty condition, the locomotive, like most of the Scottish 'Directors', has clearly been stored out of use for some time previously. This example of LNER's development of the Great Central Railway's Robinson 4-4-0 type (LNER D11) was built in 1924 by Kitsons. Bailie MacWheeble was a character in Sir Walter Scott's first novel, *Waverley,* published in 1814. One D11 Director has been preserved, albeit not a Scottish one: No. 62660 *Butler-Henderson,* the first of the class. *(Jim Oatway)*

Here is a locomotive that is still with us today, the only A2 pacific to survive, No. 60532 *Blue Peter*. It is not named after the children's TV programme but commemorates the racehorse which won the Derby and 2000 Guineas in 1939, although the TV programme has undoubtedly helped to publicise the engine. The generic class of A2s consisted of forty engines but *Blue Peter* was one of fifteen A2/3 variants designed by Peppercorn which were built in 1947–8. Initially these A2s were allocated to English depots but some were later transferred to Scotland for hauling Edinburgh-Aberdeen expresses. This photograph was taken at Perth on 1 August 1966 and No. 60532 became the last member of the class to remain in service, being withdrawn on 31 December 1966. *(Martin Jenkins/Online Transport Archive)*

With its tired appearance and traces of rust on the front bogie wheel as evident in this view at Perth shed in September 1965, Gresley A4 pacific No. 60019 *Bittern* looked as though it might not run again. However, the locomotive lived on for another year, not being withdrawn until 3 September 1966 immediately after making the last BR A4 run (a return trip between Buchanan Street, Glasgow, and Aberdeen) on the same day. No. 60019 was not in fact the last A4 to remain in stock, this dubious honour passing to No. 60024 *Kingfisher* which was not officially withdrawn until 14 September 1966. *Bittern* had better luck than *Kingfisher* though because it was bought for preservation, joining five other A4s which were saved, and has been a frequent performer on the national rail network over the last fifty years. *(Author)*

This is Gleneagles station which looks better today than it did back in August 1965 when this picture was taken of A4 No. 60024 *Kingfisher* working an Aberdeen-Glasgow express. Originally opened by the Scottish Central Railway in 1856 as Crieff Junction and renamed Gleneagles in 1912, the station was built in its current form in 1919 by the CR and ceased to be a junction on 6 July 1964 when the Crieff branch closed and the bay platform (out of picture on the left, beyond the flower beds) abandoned. The latticework on the footbridge is now revealed and considerable renovation work was undertaken in 2014 in preparation for the holding of the Ryder Cup at the nearby golf resort. The CR also built the neighbouring Gleneagles Hotel, although this opened under LMS auspices in 1924. *(Martin Jenkins/Online Transport Archive)*

The scandalous waste of money arising from the premature withdrawal of modern BR steam locomotives is epitomised in this view of Standard class 5 4-6-0 No. 73151 on Gleneagles Bank hauling an Aberdeen-Glasgow express on 19 May 1965. The locomotive entered service in April 1957 at St Rollox depot, Glasgow, and was withdrawn there in August 1966, racking up less than ten years service, despite being fitted with expensive Caprotti valve gear. The gradients around Gleneagles are significant, the 7 miles between Dunning and Gleneagles in the southerly direction, for example, varying from 1 in 89 to 1 in 121, with the summit further south of Gleneagles station. *(Alan Sainty collection)*

Heading back to the west side of Scotland we visit the NBR's Craigendoran station situated on the northern shore of the Firth of Clyde to view LNER class V3 2-6-2 tank No. 67614 with a train from Helensburgh to Glasgow. The photograph was taken on 11 April 1959 just before the North Clydeside overhead electric system was installed in preparation for the introduction of the 'Blue Electrics' in November 1960. On the left is the Craigendoran pier platform (since abandoned) and on the right is the so-called upper station which was the starting point of the West Highland Railway (absorbed by the NBR in 1908) which ran to Crianlarich, Fort William and eventually Mallaig. The upper station has since been demolished and the lower station has been reduced to a single line platform. Even the covered footbridge has been replaced.

*(Paul de Beer/Online Transport Archive)*

Also on 11 April 1959 at Craigendoran the photographer 'snapped' NBR class M/LNER class C15 4-4-2 tank No. 67460 from Glasgow's Eastfield depot. This locomotive is working the push-and-pull service on the West Highland line to Arrochar and Tarbet. A Park Royal diesel railbus took over a few months later and the service was withdrawn in June 1964 although Craigendoran and Arrochar stations remain open. This handsome Atlantic tank belonged to a class of thirty such locomotives built between 1911 and 1913 and, unusually, the NBR placed the order for their construction with the Yorkshire Engine Company, resulting in the engines being nicknamed 'Yorkies'. In this picture, the push-and-pull train is standing in the pier platform. *(Paul de Beer/Online Transport Archive)*

This is how Arrochar and Tarbet station appeared on 7 August 1962, looking towards Glasgow. Unfortunately, the Swiss-chalet style station building, which was typical of those on the West Highland Railway, has been demolished, apparently due to subsidence. However, two small buildings have been erected on the platform which are largely in keeping with the original. *(John McCann/Online Transport Archive)*

Moving closer to Glasgow, this is Wemyss Bay with Fairburn 2-6-4 tank No. 42263 departing with the 5.30pm to Glasgow Central in September 1962, a journey of some 26 miles. The line was opened in 1865 by the CR to connect with Clyde steamer services and the present station, an Edwardian masterpiece with Category A listed building status, was built in 1903. It has recently been restored to its former glory and has been served by electric trains since 1967. *(Marcus Eavis/Online Transport Archive)*

Now we are in Glasgow and on 20 May 1961 one of the Cowlairs Incline banking engines, class N15 0-6-2 No. 69183, is running light through Anniesland station on the now electrified Argyle line. The slip coupling rope operated from the cab enabling the locomotive to detach itself when pushing a train is clearly visible. Anniesland station was opened by the NBR in 1886 and was called Great Western Road, receiving its new name in 1932. The lattice girder bridge behind the locomotive crosses Great Western Road and dates from 1930 when the road was widened. The line on which the station is situated was originally the Stobcross Railway opened by the NBR in 1874 to link Maryhill with a new dock at Stobcross, later called Queen's Dock. *(Charles Firminger)*

The Cowlairs incline has a gradient of between 1 in 41 and 1 in 45 for nearly 2 miles beginning immediately outside the ex-NBR Glasgow Queens Street station and reaching almost up to Cowlairs station. In this view an unidentified class N15 0-6-2 tank is banking the Glasgow-King's Cross Queen of Scots Pullman train as diners gorge. The carriage nearest the camera is 1960-built Car No. 342, a Metro-Cammell Mark 1 Kitchen Second which formed part of this train in 1961. Next to the engine is Parlour Brake Car No. 77, a steel K type vehicle dating from 1928. *(Bruce Jenkins)*

Pinkston power station dominates this view of the Cowlairs incline on 1 October 1956. A class J36 0-6-0 shunts loaded coal trucks at the power station while class A4 4-6-2 No. 60004 *William Whitelaw* powers its way up the incline, assisted by a banking locomotive, while working the 10am train from Glasgow Queens Street to Edinburgh Waverley. The power station was built in 1901 to provide electricity to Glasgow Corporation's new tramway system and subsequently supplied power for the City's trolleybuses and Underground. The cooling tower was erected in 1954. At the time of their respective construction both the power station and the cooling tower were reputed to be the largest in Europe. The whole site was cleared in 1978. *(J.G. Todd/Online Transport Archive)*

A final look at Cowlairs incline provides a view on 16 April 1960 of class A3 4-6-2 No. 60057 *Ormonde* blotting out Pinkston power station as it makes its ascent, banked by class N15 0-6-2 tank No. 69183. Hopefully, the slip coupling on the N15 will operate, otherwise the train will have to stop at Cowlairs station for the banking engine to be detached, a not uncommon occurrence. The A3, which had been built in 1925, was based at Haymarket at the time of this picture, and lasted in service until October 1963. It was named after a racehorse which won three classic races in one year: the 2000 guineas, the Derby and the St Leger in 1886 and regarded by many as 'the horse of the century'. *(Bruce Jenkins)*

At the top of Cowlairs bank was the NBR's Cowlairs Works and a little further on was Eastfield MPD. The depot opened in 1904 but subsequently burnt down and was rebuilt in 1919. Eastfield shed remained open until November 1996 after which the site was cleared but now a new train-care facility has risen from the proverbial ashes. As for the picture, this was taken on 4 September 1965 after class A4 No. 60026 *Miles Beevor* had just completed a railtour duty. The engine was originally named *Kestrel* but in 1947 it was named after Miles Beevor who occupied a senior position in the LNER at the time. No. 60026 was withdrawn in December 1965 and moved to Crewe Works where some parts were used in the restoration of No. 60007 *Sir Nigel Gresley*. *(Author)*

In 1856 the CR built its locomotive, carriage and wagon works at St Rollox, some 2 miles from its terminus at Buchanan Street, Glasgow, and went on to build running sheds a little further on at Balornock (but normally called St Rollox). The depot closed on 7 November 1966 along with Buchanan Street station. Against the background of new high-rise flats in September 1965, a line-up of four locomotives was recorded, these being, from left to right, Nos 73107, 44931, 73146 and 73140. Three are Standard class 5 4-6-0s and one (No. 44931) is a Stanier Black Five. *(Author)*

This picture of LMS Fowler 2P 4-4-0 No. 40608 from Hurlford depot near Kilmarnock, was taken on 18 September 1959 at Glasgow St Enoch station. This was a large station, with twelve platforms, covered by two arched roofs reminiscent of the one at St Pancras in London. St Enoch had been the headquarters of the G&SWR and served towns such as Ayr, Dumfries, Kilmarnock and Stranraer. There were also some through trains to London including the Thames-Clyde Express to St Pancras via the Settle-Carlisle line. The station closed on 27 June 1966 and services were diverted to Glasgow Central. It was demolished in 1977 along with the hotel that fronted the station and a large shopping centre now stands on the site. *(John McCann/Online Transport Archive)*

Also seen on 18 September 1959 at St Enoch station, but on the opposite side, was another smart-looking LMS 2P 4-4-0 from Hurlford depot, No. 40609. Unfortunately, no examples of this type of locomotive have survived. Arguably, the National Railway Museum's preserved Midland Compound, No. 1000, bears a superficial resemblance to the 2P, apart from being larger and having outside cylinders, but to obtain a better idea of how a Midland 2P 4-4-0 looked, it is necessary to go to the Cultra Folk and Transport Museum, near Belfast in Northern Ireland, to see Northern Counties Committee No. 74 *Dunluce Castle*. *(John McCann/Online Transport Archive)*

This 'Jumbo', Polmadie-based CR Drummond 'Standard Goods' 2F 0-6-0 No. 57292, gave 75 years of service between 1886 and 1961 and sports a smart tender in this view of a shunting operation just north of Pollokshields East station, Glasgow. Immediately behind the train is the Muirhouse Sawmills & Joinery Works of Watt Torrance Ltd in Maxwell Road, which was also the location of the Pollokshields gas works, part of which is just visible behind the timber yard buildings. In the distance on the left is the Cathcart Circle line to Glasgow Central running alongside Darnley Street. The lines in the foreground exiting to the right formerly went to St Enoch. The photograph was taken in May 1959 from the rear of the Corporation Tramway Permanent Way yard in Barrland Street. *(Marcus Eavis/Online Transport Archive)*

In 1896 the G&SWR built a large engine shed at Corkerhill, Glasgow, to relieve congestion at its mainline terminus at St Enoch. This picture taken at Corkerhill depicts a BR Riddles Britannia class locomotive, No. 70044 *Earl Haig*. This locomotive had an interesting history because, on entry into service in 1953, it was fitted, as was No. 70043, with Westinghouse air brake equipment for use on braking trials on the London Midland Region. This equipment, mounted alongside the smokebox, prevented the fitting of smoke deflectors and also delayed its naming (although one member of the class of fifty-five was in fact never named). The locomotive reverted to normal Britannia condition in 1957 with the addition of deflectors and a nameplate. It was withdrawn in October 1966 and broken up but two class members are preserved in working order, Nos 70000 and 70013. *(Harry Luff/Online Transport Archive)*

Polmadie was the Glasgow depot created by the CR for the Scottish end of the WCML services from London (Euston) to Glasgow (Central), the building shown here replacing the original wooden structure in 1925. The locomotive featured is No. 46222 *Queen Mary,* the third Stanier Coronation class pacific to be built, dating from 1937. It was originally streamlined to haul the Coronation Scot train, the LMS's answer to the LNER's streamlined Coronation train hauled by A4s, but the streamlining was later removed on all those class members that were so fitted. No. 46222 was withdrawn in October 1963 but fortunately three of these magnificent Coronations/Duchesses have been preserved, Nos 46229, 46233 and 46235, the first of which has been 're-streamlined'. *(Harry Luff/Online Transport Archive)*

We are still at Polmadie for a view of a somewhat under appreciated type, typified by its external condition: the ten-strong Clan class pacific, represented here by No. 72001 *Clan Cameron*. These engines were based on the Britannia class but were lighter, with a smaller boiler, to increase route availability compared with Britannias. They were classified 6P rather than 7P, but were often given 7P work, for which, not surprisingly, they were not entirely suitable, and they were also prone to steaming difficulties. Five of the class were based at Polmadie (Nos 72000−4) and all these were withdrawn together in December 1962 after barely eleven years service. None was preserved but a new one is in the course of construction. No. 72001 has the honour of being the only pacific to work on the West Highland line, a duty it apparently performed well. *(Harry Luff/Online Transport Archive)*

**Left:** We end our visit to Polmadie with two views of a most unusual visitor, No. 601 *Kitchener,* belonging to the Longmoor Military Railway (LMR) in Hampshire. Although the Scottish Region had twenty-five ex-War Department (WD) 2-10-0s they borrowed this one in June 1957 for some two years primarily to carry out air-braked tests on Ravenscraig iron-ore workings although it was also used for normal freight workings and visited its birthplace, the North British Locomotive Co. in Glasgow, for overhaul and modifications. The other engines visible are CR 0-4-4 tank No. 55169 and Fairburn 2-6-4 tank No. 42162. Fellow LMR 2-10-0 No. 600 *Gordon* is preserved on the Severn Valley Railway and a further ex-WD one has been repatriated from Greece. **Above:** Some 8-miles east of Glasgow Central station, Fairburn tank No. 42195 from Glasgow's Dawsholm depot takes water at Baillieston while working the 7.11am to Coatbridge on 3 June 1963. The station closed on 5 October 1964 and re-opened about half a mile away on 4 October 1993. *(I.G. Todd/Online Transport Archive (two); Charles Firminger)*

In 1838 the Monkland & Kirkintilloch Railway built a workshop on land belonging to Kipps Farm, near Coatbridge, and Kipps remained the name of the engine shed on the site until its closure in January 1963. The depot was rebuilt by the NBR following its takeover of the Monkland Railways Company in 1865. On 27 July 1961 Holmes NBR class G/LNER class Y9 0-4-0 saddletank No. 68117 was dead on shed but was to remain in stock until July 1962. There were thirty-eight members of this class built between 1882 and 1899 and all but five survived to become BR assets in 1948. They were designed for dock and yard shunting, particularly over tracks with sharp curves, and were fitted with dumb buffers to cope with the different shapes and sizes of buffers fitted to wagons, particularly private-owned ones. Many Y9s such as this one were attached to small wooden tenders to increase coal capacity which was otherwise severely limited. *(Jim Oatway)*

South-west of Coatbridge is Motherwell where the CR built a depot following its absorption of the Clydesdale Junction Railway which had been formed to link Motherwell and Hamilton with Glasgow. On the same day that the photographer visited Kipps he also went to Motherwell depot where he found an example of the CR's version of the NBR's Y9 0-4-0 saddletank type, No. 56031. This is also fitted with a small tender but lacks dumb buffers. Thirty-four of these 'Pugs' belonging to CR classes 264 and 611 were built between 1885 and 1908, No. 56031 being from one of the later batches designated class 611, having been built in 1900. In this photograph, the locomotive has clearly not worked for some time although it was not officially withdrawn until April 1962. *(Jim Oatway)*

This study in rust at Motherwell was photographed on 20 July 1961. Records show that the unfortunate locomotive in question, No. 57404, was not officially withdrawn until October 1961 but clearly it has been out of use for a prolonged period prior to that. The locomotive is a CR class 711 2F 0-6-0, a type nicknamed 'Jumbos', and originally designed by Dugald Drummond (known also for his design work for the London & South Western Railway) although when No. 57404 was built in 1896, John McIntosh was CR locomotive superintendent. The class consisted of 244 engines built between 1883 and 1897, all being withdrawn between 1946 and 1962. *(Jim Oatway)*

Switching from east of Glasgow to the west coast south of Glasgow, BR Standard class 5 4-6-0 No. 73124 has just arrived at Ardrossan South Beach, probably on a St Enoch to Largs working. This former G&SWR station remains open today and the line has been electrified but the eastbound platform and buildings seen on the left were demolished in 1987. Passenger trains in both directions now use the platform at which the train is standing although the track on the left remains in situ for freight workings. This Corkerhill-based locomotive had a typically short life for this class, being 'born too late' due to impending dieselisation and lasting in service for just under ten years, from February 1956 to December 1965. *(Alan Sainty collection)*

Travelling south from Ardrossan we reach the former G&SWR station at Barassie, with its beautiful lawn and flower beds. These have long since disappeared even though the station is still open and the line from Glasgow to Ayr on the right has been electrified. The train passing under the bridge is bound for Kilmarnock but the platform on the left serving this route has since been abandoned and the track moved away from the platform edge, services no longer stopping there. Regrettably, no one using the station today could possibly imagine how wonderful it looked on 6 August 1965 when this picture was taken. *(Martin Jenkins/Online Transport Archive)*

Further down the Ayrshire coast we come to Newton-on-Ayr, on the northern outskirts of Ayr. This section of line was opened by the Glasgow, Paisley, Kilmarnock and Ayr Railway as early as 1839 and trains were running into Glasgow by the following year. On 1 July 1966, Standard class 2 2-6-0 No. 78051 passes through the station with a southbound short freight. This locomotive managed only eleven years of service, from November 1955 to November 1966 and so was only four months from withdrawal when this picture of it, in an already unkempt state, was taken. Newton-on-Ayr station remains open today served by electric trains. *(Alan Sainty collection)*

Possibly the most striking of the four preserved Scottish locomotives put back into service primarily to haul enthusiast specials was the Caledonian 4-2-2, No. 123. Built by Neilson & Co. of Glasgow in 1886 for that year's prestigious Edinburgh International Exhibition of Industry, Science & Art, it was then bought by the CR and, on withdrawal in 1935, had become the last Single to remain in service. In 1888, the engine had taken part in the Race to Scotland, a competition between the east and west coast mainlines, during which it performed impressively between Carlisle and Edinburgh. On 20 April 1962, No. 123 and the two preserved CR coaches were photographed **Left** at Ayr and **Above** at the abandoned Commondyke station which closed on 3 July 1950, located on the G&SWR's Auchinleck to Muirkirk branch. *(Charles Firminger - both)*

Standard class 5 4-6-0 No. 73079 which, as stated on the bufferbeam, is from Corkerhill depot arrives at Girvan on a Glasgow St Enoch to Stranraer train via Ayr. Category B Listed status has been awarded to the signal box and the station building, the latter being the only Art Deco station in Scotland. Surprisingly, it is not a 1930s building, having been completed by BR in 1951 following the destruction of the previous building by fire in 1946, but is based on an LMS design. The train is standing at the southern platform but most trains in both directions now use the northern platform. In this picture the track beside the water tower serving the bay platform has already been removed. The bay was used for stabling banking engines to assist trains up the 1 in 54 Glendoune Bank which starts almost immediately after the platform end.

*(Alan Sainty collection)*

This deceptively rural scene belies the fact that this is Stranraer Town station. Opened by the Portpatrick Railway in 1861, it was called simply Stranraer until renamed by BR in 1953. The station closed to passengers on 7 March 1966 and today's Stranraer station, now reached only from Ayr and no longer from Dumfries over the so-called 'Port Road', is the one previously known as Stranraer Harbour. The picture was taken on 15 April 1963 and features Carlisle-based Stanier Jubilee class 4-6-0 No. 45588 *Kashmir*. This locomotive was working a railtour which took it from Carlisle to Stranraer Town via Dumfries, Castle Douglas and Newton Stewart, ie over the 'Port Road'. No. 45588 was built by the North British Locomotive Co. in 1934 and was withdrawn on 1 May 1965. *(Charles Firminger)*

An impeccably presented CR Jumbo 0-6-0, No. 57375 dating from 1894 runs round the railtour coaches it has been hauling at Whithorn on 15 April 1963, the same train that the Jubilee locomotive pictured on the previous page was pulling. Whithorn was the terminus of the former Wigtownshire Railway branch from Newton Stewart which closed to passengers on 25 September 1950 and to freight in 1964. The Wigtownshire Railway and the Portpatrick Railway were merged in 1885 and acquired by a consortium comprising the G&SWR and its English partner, the Midland Railway, and the CR together with its English partner, the London & North Western Railway. The joint venture became the Portpatrick and Wigtownshire Joint Railway and remained as such until the Grouping when it was absorbed into the LMS. *(Charles Firminger)*

This is Castle Douglas station situated on the 'Port Road' from Dumfries to Stranraer shortly before its closure on 14 June 1965. The station was also a junction for the Kirkcudbright branch which is the destination of this westward facing train hauled by Standard class 4 2-6-0 No. 76073. The branch closed to passengers on 3 May 1965 and to freight six weeks later when the junction station closed. The Castle Douglas and Dumfries Railway (CD&DR) opened in 1859 and became the eastern section of the 'Port Road' once the Portpatrick Railway had reached Stranraer. The CD&DR was absorbed by the G&SWR in 1865. When photographed here, No. 76073 was allocated to Dumfries shed. Entering service in October 1956, it was withdrawn at Ayr depot in June 1966. *(Alan Sainty collection)*

This is Dumfries depot on 22 July 1961 with three long-term residents identifiable (the Standard on the left is unidentified). In the centre, with a member of the crew on the footplate preparing the locomotive for use, is CR Drummond 2F ('Jumbo') No. 57378, a veteran from 1894. The two engines partly visible are CR McIntosh 3F 0-6-0 tank No. 56302 built in 1904 and LMS Hughes 'Crab' 2-6-0 No. 42918 dating from 1930. This ex-G&SWR six-road engine shed was closed to steam on 2 May 1966 and demolished shortly afterwards. *(Jim Oatway)*

Pictured at Dumfries station on the same day, with smiling driver, was the station pilot, CR McIntosh 3F 0-6-0 No. 57600, built in 1900. The station was opened by the Glasgow, Dumfries and Carlisle Railway in 1848 and the line reached Kilmarnock and Glasgow two years later, the same year that the company became part of the newly-formed G&SWR. Dumfries later became a junction when the Castle Douglas and Dumfries Railway opened its route to Castle Douglas and Stranraer (the Port Road) in 1859–61 and the Dumfries, Lochmaben and Lockerbie Railway opened the Lockerbie branch in 1863, the latter becoming part of the CR. All these lines are now closed apart from the original G&SWR route. *(Jim Oatway)*

# Index